CREATIVE EDUCATION

SAINT LOUIS RAMS

JULIE NELSON

Published by Creative Education
123 South Broad Street, Mankato, Minnesota 56001
Creative Education is an imprint of The Creative Company

Designed by Rita Marshall

Photos by: Allsport USA, AP/Wide World Photos, SportsChrome

Library of Congress Cataloging-in-Publication Data

Nelson, Julie.
St. Louis Rams / by Julie Nelson.
p. cm. — (NFL today)
Summary: A history of the professional football team that began life in
Cleveland in 1937 and ended up in St. Louis after playing in Los Angeles for
nearly fifty years.
ISBN 1-58341-057-0

1. St. Louis Rams (Football team)—History—Juvenile literature. [1. St. Louis
Rams (Football team)—History. 2. Los Angeles Rams (Football team)—History.
3. Football—History.] I. Title. II. Title: Saint Louis Rams. III. Series: NFL today
(Mankato, Minn.)

GV956.S85N45   2000
796.332'64'0977866—dc21   99-015746

First edition

9 8 7 6 5 4 3 2 1

St. Louis, Missouri, is known as "the Gateway to the West." Located on the west bank of the Mississippi River, just downstream from the intersection of the Mississippi and Missouri Rivers, St. Louis has been a jumping-off point for Americans heading west ever since its founding in 1764. In the early 1800s, when the westward expansion began, St. Louis was often the first stop for explorers and settlers seeking adventure in the untamed lands beyond the Mississippi. Today, countless visitors heading west still stop in St. Louis, often to visit the famous Gateway Arch, which towers 630 feet into the sky.

Quarterback Norm Van Brocklin.

End Jim Benton racked up 1,067 receiving yards at 24 yards per catch.

St. Louis is home to the Cardinals professional baseball team and the Blues pro hockey team. The Cardinals football franchise was also headquartered in the city until 1988, when it moved to Phoenix, Arizona. After a seven-year absence, pro football returned to eastern Missouri in 1995, when the Los Angeles Rams decided to head east and make St. Louis their new home.

The Rams have a history of being on the move. The team joined the National Football League in 1937 as the Cleveland Rams. Between 1937 and 1944, the Rams had no winning seasons and finished last in the Western Division twice. Cleveland fans showed little interest in the team, and by the beginning of the 1945 season, owner Dan Reeves had made the decision to take the team west to Los Angeles. Before the move, however, the Rams spent one more year in Cleveland—and what a year it was.

DOWNFIELD WITH WATERFIELD

Bob Waterfield signed with Cleveland in 1945. Waterfield was an exceptional all-around athlete who loved throwing long passes, punting, kicking field goals, and playing defensive back as well. As a rookie, he took over the starting quarterback spot and led the Rams to four straight wins at the beginning of the season. His pinpoint passing and strong arm quickly earned him the nickname "the Rifle."

Cleveland fans began flocking to Memorial Stadium to watch Waterfield taunt opposing defenses with passes to his favorite target—All-Pro end Jim Benton. Then, late in the season, with the Rams in first place, Waterfield got hurt. With

Explosive receiver and punt returner Az-zahir Hakim.

only two games left, the Rams needed one victory to claim the Western Division championship.

In the locker room before the next game, a team trainer examined Waterfield's injury and gave Rams coach Adam Walsh the bad news. "It's torn rib muscles," the trainer said. "You can't use him today."

"The heck you can't!" Waterfield exploded. "Tape me up and give me a shot." His chest wrapped in tape, Waterfield took the field and proceeded to hit Benton with 10 passes for 303 yards as the Rams defeated Detroit 28–21. As champions of the Western Division with a 9–1 record, the Rams next hosted the Washington Redskins in the NFL title game.

The temperature on the day of the game was below freezing, and an icy wind whipped across the frozen field. "It was so cold," Waterfield said, "I remember thinking at the time, 'How do those guys hold onto the ball?' I didn't have any trouble, but then I didn't have to catch it."

Waterfield did everything else that day, however—passing, running, and kicking extra points. His extraordinary performance, which included touchdown passes of 37 and 53 yards, capped a remarkable season. The Rams won 15–14, Waterfield was named the NFL's Most Valuable Player, and Cleveland fans roared their approval. The world champion Rams, however, were on their way west.

Los Angeles immediately fell in love with its new team, and the club responded by finishing second in the division in 1946 with a 6–4–1 record. Over the next four years, the Los Angeles Rams established themselves as one of the most exciting offensive teams in the NFL. In one game in 1948, the Rams fell behind the Philadelphia Eagles 28–0, but Wa-

1 9 4 6

*Bob Waterfield ri-
fled the ball to his
receivers for 17
touchdowns.*

terfield refused to give up. He shredded the Eagles' secondary with passes to Bob Shaw and sensational rookie Tom Fears to lead his team to a 28–28 tie. Fans were shocked, especially in Philadelphia.

Tom Fears led the NFL in receptions his rookie year and again the following season. The Rams' air assault was already awesome, but it got even better in 1949 when the team acquired a fleet-footed halfback named Elroy "Crazy Legs" Hirsch, who also played wide receiver. Waterfield then had Fears, Hirsch, and Shaw as prime passing targets, and he used them with devastating results. The Rams won their first six games in 1949, then captured the Western Division title before being blanked 14–0 by the Eagles in the NFL championship game.

With the addition of talented rookie Elroy Hirsch, the Rams averaged 30 points per game.

The Rams' offensive power peaked the following season with the addition of ex-Army star running back Glenn Davis. Waterfield shared quarterbacking duties with a strong-armed, second-year sensation named Norm Van Brocklin, and the twosome wreaked havoc on the league. The Rams racked up an NFL-record 466 points and 64 touchdowns in 1950. They also scored 70 points in a single game—a 70–28 romp over the Baltimore Colts.

During the season, Van Brocklin emerged as the team's passing leader, and rumors circulated that Waterfield might be traded. Owner Dan Reeves, however, laughed at the idea. "I wouldn't trade Bob for the Brooklyn Bridge, with any player you name thrown in."

With Waterfield on the field, no lead was safe against the Rams. In one game, the Green Bay Packers watched a 28–6 lead evaporate as Waterfield led three touchdown drives,

Record-setting passer Jim Everett.

Swift wide receiver Henry Ellard.

Norm Van Brocklin did double duty, starring as both passer and punter.

then kicked a field goal to give the Rams a 30–28 win. After the amazing comeback, one reporter wrote, "Games such as [those] the Rams and the Rifle played on Sunday are the kind that set professional football apart, give it that extra touch of quality which makes it the finest game in the land."

The Rams finished first in their division, then met the Cleveland Browns in the 1950 NFL championship. The game was played in Cleveland, a homecoming of sorts for the Rams. But the homecoming was spoiled in the final minute of the game as a Cleveland field goal gave the Browns a 30–28 edge and the championship.

In 1951, the Rams were the NFL's top-scoring team for the second straight season and won their third straight division title. In the 1951 league championship game, the Rams battled the Browns again. Waterfield started the game and passed and kicked the Rams to a 14–10 lead in the third quarter. The Browns then rallied to tie the game at 17–17. But with three minutes left, Van Brocklin came into the game and unleashed a 73-yard touchdown pass to Tom Fears, giving Los Angeles a 24–17 win.

Waterfield retired after the 1952 season. Van Brocklin seemed to have emerged as the clear starting quarterback, but his moment alone in the spotlight didn't last long. Soon, a younger passer named Bill Wade was also getting a lot of playing time. The joke in Los Angeles was that the most popular player for the Rams was the backup quarterback. If Van Brocklin was on the field, the fans called for Wade, and vice versa.

Van Brocklin was traded to the Eagles in 1958, and the Rams began to lose their position as a top team in the Western Division. They won the division title in 1955 and finished tied for second place in 1958, but those would be the only winning seasons for the team from 1955 to 1965.

ROMAN TO THE RESCUE

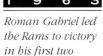

Roman Gabriel led the Rams to victory in his first two games as starter.

Rams officials searched far and wide for a quarterback who could drive a team the way Waterfield and Van Brocklin had. In 1962, Los Angeles used its first draft pick to select North Carolina State quarterback Roman Gabriel.

In 1966, owner Dan Reeves also hired George Allen as coach. Allen vowed to make the Rams a winner. "I want to win today," he said. "I don't like waiting. It's not my style to plan for the future. To me, the future is now."

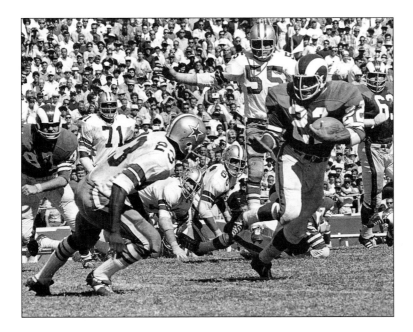

A backfield star of the '60s, Dick Bass.

Likewise, Roman Gabriel had never enjoyed waiting on the bench. "In high school and college, not only was I a starter, I was a star," he recalled. "But when I became a pro, I was on the bench, a forgotten man. It hurt my love of the game, my dedication, and my confidence."

Gabriel decided to play out the option year of his contract in 1966, then sign with another team. Allen, however, had plans for the quarterback. "Don't play out your option," Allen told Gabriel. "Sign with the Rams and I'll make you my regular quarterback." It was an offer Gabriel couldn't refuse.

Behind a suddenly more confident Gabriel, the Rams finished 11–1–2 in 1967. Jack Snow had emerged as an excellent wide receiver, while halfback Dick Bass revved up the Rams' running game. On defense, Los Angeles had perhaps the best line in the NFL. Dubbed "the Fearsome Foursome," Rosey Grier, Merlin Olsen, Deacon Jones, and Lamar Lundy thrilled fans and throttled opposing quarterbacks. "Until we came along," Olsen said, "most fans only looked to offensive players for excitement. The emergence of our line brought some attention over to the defense."

The much-improved Rams won their division in 1967 but lost 28–7 to the Green Bay Packers, the eventual Super Bowl champions, in the first round of the playoffs. Despite the loss, Gabriel had clearly emerged as a star. "I'm a better quarterback now than I was at this time last year," he told reporters at the end of the 1967 season. "The big thing is that the team believes in me."

In 1968, the Rams continued their climb to excellence with a 10–3–1 regular-season record. They did even better in 1969, winning the division again with an 11–3 record.

Kevin Greene reminded fans of the Fearsome Foursome.

Jackie Slater anchored the Rams' offensive line for 20 seasons.

Gabriel tossed 24 touchdown passes and was named the NFL's Most Valuable Player.

Still, Gabriel knew that success came only through team effort. "The longer I play," he said, "the more I realize that the quarterback is just one of 40 men on a pro team. He is no better than the people around him. I'm a successful quarterback because I'm on a successful team."

The Rams had high hopes as they entered the playoffs in 1969. However, the Minnesota Vikings knocked them out in the Western Conference title game, 23–20. It would be the Rams' last playoff appearance for four years.

In 1973, Chuck Knox took over as the Rams' head coach. A new quarterback, John Hadl, and a new wide receiver, Harold Jackson, energized the offense, and the Rams returned to their winning ways again. From 1973 to 1979, the Rams won the NFC Western Division every year.

Knox built his team around a solid defense keyed by linebacker Isiah Robertson and two Jacks: defensive end Jack Youngblood and linebacker Jack Reynolds. On offense, Lawrence McCutcheon and Cullen Bryant carried the ball behind an offensive line that included two All-Pros, guard Dennis Harrah and tackle Jackie Slater.

In spite of all his success, though, Knox could not lead the Rams to the Super Bowl. In 1978, he was replaced as coach by Ray Malavasi, and in 1979, the Rams made it all the way to the Super Bowl at last. Behind young quarterback Vince Ferragamo, the Rams took a 19–18 lead over heavily favored Pittsburgh, but the Steelers battled back to down Los Angeles 32–19.

1 9 7 5

End Jack Youngblood was named the NFL Defensive Player of the Year.

The Rams' hard-hitting defense (pages 18-19).

Georgia Frontiere became the only woman to own an NFL franchise.

When John Robinson became the Rams' head coach in 1983, the first thing he did was draft Eric Dickerson, a powerful 6-foot-3 halfback out of Southern Methodist University. During training camp, however, Robinson thought Dickerson wasn't trying as hard as he could, and he screamed at the rookie to work harder. Robinson finally realized that Dickerson was so naturally talented that it only looked as if he wasn't trying.

"He made no noise when he ran," Robinson recalled. "If you were blind, he could run right by you, and I don't think you'd know he was there unless you felt the wind."

Dickerson shocked the NFL by rushing for 1,808 yards on 390 carries in 1983, the most yards a rookie had ever amassed. Dickerson's 120 points also led the Rams and was a key factor in their return to the playoffs as a Wild Card team with a 9–7 record.

In his sophomore season, Dickerson rushed for 2,105 yards, the best NFL single-season mark ever. He also led the league in rushing in 1983, 1984, and 1986. In only five seasons with the Rams, Dickerson became the Rams' all-time leading rusher with 7,245 yards.

In 1985, Los Angeles went 11–5 in the regular season and took on the Chicago Bears in the NFC championship game. Unfortunately for Rams fans, the Bears' powerful defense ganged up on Dickerson as the "Monsters of the Midway" dominated the Rams 24–0.

Throughout the 1980s, the Rams had been searching for a talented quarterback to complement their strong running game. In 1986, the Rams traded with the Houston Oilers for quarterback Jim Everett. Backing up Oilers great Warren Moon, Everett knew he'd see little playing time in Houston. The trade was just what Everett was looking for and just what the Rams needed.

Coach Robinson also brought in Ernie Zampese as the team's new offensive coordinator. It took a season, but Zampese's guidance did the trick. In 1988, Everett led the NFL with 31 touchdown passes and threw for nearly 4,000 yards, while running back Greg Bell ran for 1,212 yards and 16 touchdowns. One of Everett's prime targets was Henry Ellard, who grabbed 86 passes and scored 10 touchdowns. Ellard, who played for the Rams from 1983 to 1994, would eventually become the team's all-time leading receiver.

Head coach John Robinson guided the Rams to an 11–5 record.

All-Pro quarterback Jim Everett.

21

Eric Dickerson averaged 1,450 rushing yards per season.

Everett's ambition was simple. "I just want to be remembered at some time as being the best quarterback the Rams have had," he said, "and that won't come easy." Everett enjoyed another banner year in 1989, when he passed for more than 4,000 yards and led the Rams to the NFC championship game. The powerful San Francisco 49ers, however, then crushed Los Angeles 30–3.

Linebacker Kevin Greene led the Rams in sacks (13) for the third straight season.

FROM L.A. TO ST. LOUIS

As a team, the Rams seemed to run out of steam after their sensational 1989 season. In 1990, they slumped to a disappointing 5–11 record. The next two seasons, the Rams finished dead last in their division.

As they began rebuilding, the Rams used their first-round draft pick in 1992 to acquire defensive tackle Sean Gilbert from Pittsburgh University. Despite his size (6-foot-5 and 315 pounds), Gilbert was blessed with amazing speed. He could sprint 40 yards in 4.5 seconds, and even though he was often double-teamed in his rookie year, his quickness enabled him to collect 10.5 sacks in 1993.

The next year, the Rams drafted Jerome Bettis out of Notre Dame. Bettis, a 5-foot-11 and 243-pound running back, had both a powerful inside game and speedy moves to the outside. He exploded onto the scene, rushing for 1,429 yards to finish second in the NFL and win Rookie of the Year honors.

Bettis's battering style earned him comparisons to another NFL great, former Houston Oilers back Earl Campbell. But Bettis was as shifty as he was powerful. "The thing about Jerome that's so crazy is he's so deceptive," said former Eagles running back Ricky Watters, who played with Bettis at Notre Dame. "You look at him and think, 'Oh, this is a big guy. I've just got to slow him up, knock his legs out from under him.' But he has great balance and a lot of speed once he gets going."

With the help of the Rams' offensive line, Bettis recorded back-to-back 1,000-yard rushing seasons in 1993 and 1994. This line included veteran guard Jackie Slater and two-time All-Pro Tom Newberry. Slater, a tower of power for the Rams from 1976 to 1995, retired having played in more games (259) than any offensive lineman in NFL history.

Still, the Rams stumbled in 1994, especially at the quarterback position. Chris Miller emerged as the new starter after the departure of Everett, but he could not lead the Rams out

1 9 9 4

Linebacker Shane Conlan led the team in tackles, making 106 stops.

Jerome Bettis pummeled tacklers with his powerful running.

of the cellar. The team was in turmoil, finishing last in the NFC again with an embarrassing 4–12 record and ending the year with a seven-game losing skid. Fan support was at an all-time low. Before the 1995 season, the team decided to make some big changes.

The first thing Rams management did was replace coach Chuck Knox—who had returned to the Rams in 1992—with Rich Brooks, a 17-year coaching veteran at Oregon State. Then, in early 1995, Rams owner Georgia Frontiere announced that the Rams were leaving Los Angeles and moving east to St. Louis.

Linebacker Roman Phifer made 170 tackles—the second-highest total in Rams history.

REBIRTH OF THE RAMS

St. Louis fans were thrilled to again have an NFL team, and the Rams were happy with their new home. "This environment is so much more positive for our team," said Brooks. "It's what we really needed."

Nearly 60,000 St. Louis fans packed Busch Stadium to greet the team on opening day in 1995, and the Rams didn't disappoint them. With Chris Miller firmly in control at the quarterback spot, the Rams scored a 17–14 upset victory over a strong Packers team. St. Louis won its next four games as well before its unbeaten streak was snapped by the Indianapolis Colts.

When the season had started, the Rams thought that they would face a major weakness in the pass-catching department. The team was pleasantly surprised to find that second-year wide receiver Isaac Bruce was more than ready to meet that challenge. "I trained a whole lot harder and with a lot

Perennial 1,000-yard rusher Marshall Faulk (pages 26-27).

Halfback Amp Lee led the St. Louis offense with 825 receiving yards.

more passion in the off-season, because I knew I was going to be the man," Bruce said.

Bruce proved to be a bright spot as the Rams faltered in the second half of the season. He had one of the best receiving seasons in NFL history with 119 receptions, 1,781 yards, and 13 touchdowns, setting new team records for both receptions and yardage.

Bruce remained a constant in 1996, contributing another 1,338 receiving yards. The faces around him, however, were changing. Running back Jerome Bettis had moved on to Pittsburgh, and a trio of rookies had been drafted to rejuvenate the Rams' offense—running back Lawrence Phillips, receiver Eddie Kennison, and quarterback Tony Banks.

After a 6–10 finish in 1996, Rams ownership hired a new head coach. Rich Brooks was replaced by Dick Vermeil, who had last served as an NFL coach in 1982 with Philadelphia. The team also had a new on-field leader in 1997—Tony Banks, who started every game and finished the season with 3,254 passing yards. His favorite targets were Bruce and newly acquired running back Amp Lee. Despite some strong individual performances, St. Louis again finished 6–10. The franchise's shakeup continued.

In 1998, top rushing threat Lawrence Phillips left St. Louis. Although Amp Lee, Eddie Kennison, and Ricky Proehl stepped up to improve the receiving corps, the Rams struggled to move the ball on the ground. The Rams' main claim to respectability in 1998 was their defense, led by safety Billy Jenkins, linebacker Mike Jones, and defensive end Kevin Carter.

Desperate to secure a top-notch running back to rejuvenate its sagging offense, St. Louis traded several draft picks to Indianapolis in the off-season for explosive runner Marshall Faulk. A remarkable athlete, Faulk had played as a quarterback, running back, end, wide receiver, and defensive player during high school before starring as a halfback in college. As a professional, Faulk had run for more than 1,000 yards in four of his first five seasons with the Colts.

"What sets him apart from everybody else is that he can go from a standing start to full speed faster than anybody I've ever seen," said former Indianapolis head coach Ted Marchibroda. "When he runs the ball and is forced to hesitate, his next step is full-speed."

St. Louis continued to bolster its offense by drafting swift wide receiver Torry Holt of North Carolina State in the first round of the 1999 NFL draft. After a disappointing third season with the Rams, Tony Banks was traded and replaced by former Redskins quarterback Trent Green.

Powerful end Kevin Carter led the Rams defense with an NFL-best 17 sacks.

1999 proved to be a season of magic for the St. Louis Rams. At the heart of that magic was the improbable story of quarterback Kurt Warner. Only a few years earlier, Warner—unable to catch on with any NFL team—had worked for minimum wage in an Iowa grocery store. He later played in a small, indoor football league in the Midwest. But when Trent Green suffered a season-ending injury, the Rams reluctantly called Warner up to the NFL as their starter.

The 28-year-old Warner amazed fans and experts one week at a time with his accurate passing and smart decision-making. With the support of Faulk (who set a new NFL record with 2,429 total yards from scrimmage) and a crew of speedy receivers, Warner led the suddenly explosive Rams to a 13–3 record and the NFC West championship. After

Quarterback Kurt Warner, the NFL's 1999 MVP.

A cornerback's nightmare, receiver Isaac Bruce.   31

Swift and athletic defensive back Dre' Bly was expected to blossom into a star.

throwing 41 touchdown passes, Warner was named the league's Most Valuable Player. "I told our team we could win with Kurt," Coach Vermeil said. "I didn't expect that he'd play well enough that we'd win *because* of him."

In the second round of the playoffs, the Rams beat the Minnesota Vikings in a 49–37 shootout. A week later, the Rams captured the NFC championship by holding off Tampa Bay for an 11–6 victory. The win set up a "Cinderella" Super Bowl matchup—the Rams against the Tennessee Titans, another team that had risen from mediocrity to sudden greatness.

In the Super Bowl, St. Louis built a 16–0 lead, only to have Tennessee come back to tie the score. The Rams finally struck again late in the fourth quarter, as Warner hit Isaac Bruce with a 73-yard touchdown pass. In a thrilling finish, Rams linebacker Mike Jones pulled down a Titans receiver on the Rams' one-yard line as time expired to preserve a 23–16 victory. The city of St. Louis had its first NFL championship, and the Rams franchise had its first title since 1951.

Although Coach Vermeil decided to retire after the Super Bowl victory, Warner and St. Louis hope to continue adding chapters to their amazing story. With a wealth of offensive talent and the backing of some of the NFL's loudest fans, today's Rams are hoping to form the NFL's next dynasty.